Mountain
Lion
Alert

*Safety Tips for Yourself, Your Children, Your
Pets, and Your Livestock in Lion Country*

Steven Torres

FALCON®

Helena, Montana

© 1997 Falcon® Publishing Co., Inc.,
Helena and Billings, Montana

10 9 8 7 6 5 4 3 2 1

Printed in Canada.

Illustrations by Todd Telander
Cover photo by Mike A. Anich

Library of Congress Cataloging-in-Publication Data

Torres, Steven.
    Mountain lion alert / Steven Torres.
        p.   cm.
    Includes bibliographical references.
    ISBN 1-56044-583-1 (pbk.)
    1. Pumas. 2. Lion attacks—Prevention. I. Title.
QL737.C232T675   1997
599.75'24—dc21   97-17551
                                                          CIP

CAUTION
    Outdoor recreation can be dangerous, including recreating and
living in mountain lion country. Everyone who goes into mountain lion
country assumes some risk and responsibility for his or her own actions
and safety.
    The information contained in this book is a summary of the author's
personal experiences, research, review of existing literature on mountain
lion–human conflicts, and conversations with many mountain lion
experts. This book has been reviewed by mountain lion experts prior to
publication. However, neither this book (nor any other book) can assure
your safety from mountain lions. Nor can this book (or any other book)
replace sound judgment and good decision-making skills, which will
greatly reduce the risks of going into mountain lion country.
    Learn as much as possible from this book and other sources of
information, and prepare for the unexpected. Be safe and cautious. The
reward will be a safer and more enjoyable experience.

For my girls

Contents

Preface

Let's establish some perspective on the problem of mountain lions attacking people. First, attacks by mountain lions on people are rare. Indeed, hundreds of mountain lion encounters, not attacks, are reported each year. During the past 100 years, approximately 66 attack incidents have been recorded in North America (the United States and Canada), resulting in 15 human fatalities. Most dramatically, 75 percent of these incidents have occurred since 1970. During the past 10 years, between 1 and 5 mountain lion attacks on humans have been reported yearly in the United States and Canada. However, rather than dismiss these events as statistically remote, using examples like "you are more likely to die from bee stings or lightning," I believe it is more important to educate readers about the presence of these large predators and to foster an awareness that helps the public understand and respect these animals as part of our wildlife heritage. I do not intend this book to be a thorough description covering all aspects of the natural history of these fascinating and magnificent animals, but I will attempt to answer the primary questions that I am often asked or ask myself, and I will provide a guide to "alert" the reader to the presence of these animals. In addition, I will present the conservation challenge that we need to meet in order to allow mountain lions to persist in the rapidly changing West.

Acknowledgments

My first experience studying large mammals occurred while I was completing my master's degree in wildlife ecology at the University of Arizona (Tucson). In 1981 I accepted a university research position studying desert bighorn sheep in the Little Harquahala Mountains of southwestern Arizona. Dr. Paul Krausman coordinated the larger project that included several mountain ranges in which desert mule deer and bighorn sheep were to be monitored. This research represented my first opportunity to study large mammals and my first opportunity to see mountain lion sign, kills, and eventually a brief glimpse of the great cat. I was hired because of my demonstrated ability to survive the harsh conditions of the Sonoran desert, despite my poor reputation with cholla cactus and vehicles. For this experience I am grateful, and my heart will always be in the southwestern deserts.

After a brief and painful hiatus at UCLA, where I studied biostatistics, earning another master's degree, I returned to the wildlife profession and accepted a position coordinating the statewide management programs for bighorn sheep and mountain lions for the California Department of Fish and Game. This experience has given me an appreciation for wildlife management beyond biology and research. California's bighorn sheep management program is relatively well funded, has an active research program, and employs trained and dedicated professionals. But mountain lion management has a highly political history that most recently has been resolved at the ballot box. Currently, no hunting is allowed, no funding is provided, the public has a high level of emotional and political interest, and we know very little about the status of these animals in most regions of the state. The diversity of opinion regarding the "problems" associated with mountain lions and the proposed solutions is impressive and bewildering, and in part motivates this book.

In particular, I want to credit individuals and

projects that have provided me the opportunity to study and learn about large mammals. These individuals include Arizonans Dr. Paul Krausman and Dr. Norm Smith (University of Arizona), Dr. Rick Seegmiller (deceased), Mr. John Hervert and Mr. Bob Henry (Arizona Game and Fish Department), and Californians Dr. Vern Bleich, Mr. Bill Clark, Mr. Terry Mansfield, Mr. Bob Teagle, Mr. Doug Updike, and Mr. Dick Weaver (California Department of Fish and Game), Mr. Dave Fjeline (Placer County), and Dr. John Wehausen (White Mountain Research Station). Dr. Holley Ernest (University of California, Davis), Ms. Jeannie Clark (California Watchable Wildlife Project), and Mr. Doug Janz (Ministry of Environment, Lands, and Parks, British Columbia) all shared important information and discussion regarding mountain lions. Also, I would like to thank my reviewers: Dr. Vern Bleich, Dr. Lee Fitzhugh, Mr. Dave Fjeline, Mr. Doug Padley, and Dr. John Wehausen. Ms. Barbara Torres, my wife, contributed greatly toward focusing my tangential ramblings.

Thanks to Russ Schneider and Rick Newby at Falcon Publishing for managing the production of this book, and to designer Janet Bukantis and production editor Arik Ohnstad for their efforts. Copy editor Eileen Gallagher should also be mentioned, as should Todd Telander, who provided the illustrations.

State and provincial wildlife agencies should be credited for the numerous brochures and reports they offer to the public to provide education and safety information. Much of this information is used in this book.

Special thanks to my two main "partners in crime," Dr. Vern Bleich and Dr. John Wehausen, with whom I have spent countless memorable hours in the field considering bighorn sheep, mountain lions, and the interesting challenges of studying large mammals in a state that is profoundly diverse both ecologically and politically. They are my colleagues, friends, and teachers, and they have supported the challenge to "make a difference" for wildlife.

The Mountain Lion Controversy

THE TRUTH IS SOMEWHERE IN BETWEEN

Pumas are like a light breeze: when one is present, you know it; you can feel it, but you don't see it.
—JOHN SEIDENSTICKER, 1991

Have you ever been in the outdoors and felt that you were being watched? Whether backpacking in the high country, mountain biking through golden hills, or exploring the wilds of a rural creek, you have probably crossed paths with an incredible variety of animals without even noticing—maybe even an elusive mountain lion. A mountain lion? How could you not have known? Because, although these animals are a relatively common predator in the western United States, they are masterfully secretive and ordinarily very wary of people.

The mountain lion, also commonly referred to as cougar, panther, and puma, has long evoked mystery, fear, respect, and fascination. Native Americans, early settlers, scientists, and the modern public have all been fascinated by mountain lions, yet they vary in their tolerance for these predators. Among North and Central American native peoples, mountain lions were culturally important as spiritual icons and were both respected and feared. On the other hand, during the nineteenth century, ranchers and western townspeople alike saw the mountain lion as an obstacle to settlement of the frontier. Our conflict with mountain lions continues today as we face the issues of the lions' impact on domestic livestock and pets and public concern about an alarming number of attacks on people.

The "controversy" regarding mountain lions is

fueled by speculation and emotion. And potential solutions to mountain lion and human conflicts are greatly oversimplified. Many people believe that these animals are extremely rare or even endangered, while others think that the numbers of mountain lions are increasing uncontrollably and pose a threat to lives and property. The truth is somewhere in between. Mountain lions are predators at the top of the food chain and, as a rule, are fewer in number than their prey. They are not biologically threatened or endangered. However, in regions heavily impacted by human development such as southern California, mountain lions have lost habitat and their historic distributions are now somewhat fragmented. Their prey populations have been similarly disturbed. Furthermore, we are seeing the rather invisible boundaries that once divided the wild from the city now blurring.

Is the number of mountain lions increasing uncontrollably? No. Predators are part of the "ecological system" that has built-in checks to ensure that their numbers reflect the availability of resources that are essential to their survival, such as food (prey) and cover (habitat). Many people do not understand that mountain lions have co-evolved with their prey over thousands of years. However, the relationships between and circumstances influencing predators and prey are varied. While some research tells us that predator populations generally do not control the abundance of their prey, other research has shown that predators may significantly influence prey numbers. There are no simple rules.

Most of what we think we know about the relationships between predators and prey describes undisturbed ecological systems. Humans, on the other hand, have dramatically altered the western hemisphere during the past 200 years, and ecological relationships are now a complex mix of natural and "human-induced" factors. California, for example, has changed dramatically during the past 100 years, and what happens there may forecast the future of the mountain lion's fate in many other western states.

Until recently (through the early 1960s), state and federal bounty systems provided incentive to kill mountain lions. So, quite naturally, many biologists believe that the subsequent elimination of the bounty programs led to dramatic increases in the distribution and abundance of mountain lions during the past 30 years. However, the end of these programs also coincided with incredible human population increases in California. In addition, the abundance of non-native wild pigs, domestic animals, and pets has provided "alternate prey" for mountain lions and further complicated the picture. Without question, some areas of California have been more heavily impacted by human activity than others, and mountain lions may be more adaptable to or even tolerant of human activity than we have realized.

Several theories may explain recent increases in human/mountain lion conflicts. I speculate that mountain lion and human activity have crossed a threshold. If so, attacks are now inevitable. Indeed, my research in California has shown that most attacks on people and pets have occurred along the "urban fringe," where human development and recreation in mountain lion habitat is highest. On the other hand, areas that see high levels of mountain lion attacks on livestock are not areas of high human development, but rather areas where mountain lion habitat is plentiful. The attacks in these areas may represent an increase in mountain lion numbers and distribution. Different problems, different areas, and probably different solutions.

Mountain Lion Attacks

WHY DO MOUNTAIN LIONS
ATTACK PEOPLE?

We don't know, but everyone has a theory. Often, I see it postulated that when mountain lions attack, they are protecting young or defending kills. But mountain lions are not known to do this, as bears are. The only common observation is that humans are sometimes attacked, killed, and consumed as prey. Mountain lions use stealth in human attacks, as they do for other prey, and most individuals attacked have little warning. Do mountain lions somehow confuse humans with prey? Does running or quick movement stimulate the predator response? But then, if running and prey confusion are the only important factors, shouldn't we be seeing more attacks?

Do mountain lions habituate to the presence of humans and lose their wariness? This is unclear because attacks have occurred in both relatively remote and populated areas. California and British Columbia currently have the "lion's share" of attacks, and yet the two regions appear more different than similar with regard to densities of people and recreational activity. High numbers of mountain lions are found in both regions, though, and attacks do occur more frequently in areas of higher human activity.

Whatever complex interaction of factors may be involved, mountain lions periodically attack people. We may never fully understand why. Even if we did know, could wildlife agencies do anything to prevent attacks? Probably not. However, there is concern and some evidence to suggest that once a mountain lion has attacked, it may attack again. It is this unusual behavior that justifies a particular mountain lion's removal as a threat to public safety.

WHAT IS THE PROFILE OF MOUNTAIN LIONS THAT ATTACK PEOPLE?

There is not a stereotypical "man killing" mountain lion. Both male and female mountain lions are equally represented in accounts of mountain lions attacking people. Interestingly, this is in contrast to records that report more male mountain lions killing livestock. Young mountain lions (2 to 3 years old) are quite highly represented in accounts of human attack incidents when transient or dispersing into new areas.

ATTACK SUMMARY ... PEOPLE AND PLACES

In 1991, Dr. Paul Beier (University of Northern Arizona) published a summary of verified mountain lion attacks on people that have occurred in North America since 1890. He found that most attack victims were children 16 years or younger and that the majority were not accompanied by adults. He also found that the majority of adult victims were alone and that most victims did not see the mountain lion before the attack. Victims' efforts at fighting back by using a stick, rock, jacket, knife, bare hands, or shouting were often successful.

I have updated this attack history (through 1996—see Table 1, page 25) and divided it into 2 periods to cover attacks both during and after the bounty programs. The current period (1970 to the present) includes the elimination of bounties and higher levels of protection for mountain lions, coincident with a rapid increase in the human population. This is the period in which we have observed significant increases in mountain lion and human numbers, urban development, and recreation in the western United States and Canada. A total of 66 incidents that resulted in 59 injuries and 15 deaths were documented. It is clear that most of these incidents (75 percent) occurred after 1970. Why? More people? More lions? Or both? Likely both. Unfortunately, causes and circumstances have varied dramatically, and if there is anything researchers have learned about mountain lions, it is that there are no simple rules.

Surprisingly, more than one-half (52 percent) of attack incidents have occurred in British Columbia, the majority on Vancouver Island. However, attacks in California have occurred during the past 10 years at a rate equal to that of British Columbia, with the 2 regions reporting 8 and 9 incidents respectively. California, with its high human densities, has had a complete moratorium on mountain lion hunting since 1972, while British Columbia has a significant hunting program and much lower human densities. Mountain lion populations appear to be flourishing under both management scenarios. Clearly, hunting is not threatening mountain lion populations. Is hunting an effective solution to public safety problems? What is common to both regions is that lion attacks occurred in areas where mountain lions are not hunted; however, these areas are also not particularly suited to hunting.

REPORTING ENCOUNTERS—
RESPONSE AND INFORMATION

There is a legitimate concern that, once a mountain lion has threatened, exhibited unusual behavior toward, or attacked a person, it may present a serious risk. Always report unusual sightings or encounters to wildlife officials. Make a note of the time of day, specific location, and the behavior of the mountain lion. If you are uncertain whether your incident is of concern, call your regional wildlife agency for an assessment. The agency may be able to provide additional safety information and probably can provide you with local reports of mountain lion activity in your area.

After an attack, it is important to have someone contact wildlife and other safety officers (law enforcement) immediately. Timing is critical. The site should not be trampled since it has "clues" that experienced animal damage control agents will need to pursue and destroy the mountain lion. Wildlife enforcement officers will secure the scene to prevent additional injuries.

TABLE 1. *Summary of mountain lion attacks in North America (1890–1996)*

Time Period	State/Province	Attack Incidents	Humans Injured	Humans Killed
1890-1969	Alberta	1	1	0
	British Columbia	12	12	1
	California	2	0	3
	Texas	1	1	0
	Washington	1	0	1
	Subtotal	17	14	5
1970-1996	Alberta	2	2	0
	Arizona	2	2	0
	British Columbia	24	22	5
	California	8	7	2
	Colorado	4	3	1
	Montana	2	1	1
	Nevada	1	1	0
	New Mexico	1	0	1
	Texas	4	5	0
	Washington	1	2	0
	Subtotal	49	45	10
1890-1996	Total	66	59	15

The Mountain Lion: A Pure Predator

With its uncanny skill as a killer and its vast range, greatly exceeding that of the jaguar, [the mountain lion] may be recognized as the leading predator of the New World.—STANLEY P. YOUNG, 1946

NATURAL HISTORY AND ECOLOGY

The mountain lion is one of the largest carnivores (flesh eaters) in North America. Other large carnivores—bears, for example—are omnivorous, meaning they eat both plants and animals. Mountain lions, on the other hand, are the largest "pure" carnivore in North America and are marvelously adapted for killing prey that are often larger than themselves. Mountain lions belong to the cat family (Felidae). They are characterized by a round head with a shortened muzzle, and have excellent depth perception. The mountain lion's specialized jaw limits movement to one plane for maximum precision in the occlusion of molars and premolars. These teeth, collectively referred to as "carnassial teeth," are specially adapted to better perform their primary purpose—shearing meat. Mountain lions' elongated canine teeth are adapted to hold and immobilize prey. Mountain lions' claws are sharp and attached to the outer toe bones which are ordinarily folded back (retracted) into a skin-and-fur sheath. A ligament holds the toe bone in a retracted position to protect the claws from unnecessary wear. When a small flexor muscle in the foot contracts, the claw is extended or "protracted."

Members of the cat family are found worldwide and have traditionally been divided into three main subfamilies: 1) the large cats (lions, jaguars, leopards, and tigers); 2) the small cats (including mountain lions); and 3) the cheetah. Mountain lions are the largest members of the "small cat" subfamily, which also includes bobcats, lynx, and numerous Central and South American, European, Asian, and African cats. However, this classification among and within groups remains controversial, as each of the cat subfamilies is very diverse and contains numerous further distinct subgroups (genera).

The species name for mountain lion is *Puma concolor* (recently changed from *Felis concolor*). Mountain lions are the largest native cat in North America. In the western hemisphere, only jaguars *(Panthera onca)* are larger, but they do not occur north of Mexico, although both recent and historical accounts suggest that jaguars venture, though rarely, into the borderlands of the southwestern United States. The word *puma* is of early South American origin and means "mountain lion"; *concolor* is Latin for "one color." Indeed, the coloration of mountain lions is singularly plain, though individuals can vary in color from gray-brown to tawny (yellowish) to red-brown.

Mountain lions are solitary animals. Males and females pair only briefly to mate. Both male and female home ranges are large. In areas where deer do not make extensive seasonal movements, female mountain lion home ranges are often less than 40 square miles (100 square kilometers) in size, and although home ranges may overlap, females tend to avoid each other. Male mountain lion home ranges are larger than those of females and are often several hundred square miles. Typically, the home range of a male mountain lion will overlap several female home ranges, but only minimally overlap those of other males. Home range size and degree of overlap varies dramatically for mountain lions in different habitats, and depends on seasonal distribution, density of prey, and landscape features such as vegetation and topography, which provide essential hiding cover for acquiring prey. The broad and relatively contiguous distribution of these cats makes mountain lion populations difficult to delimit.

Female mountain lions may come into breeding condition any time of year, and so kittens can be born year-round. Mountain lions demonstrate no clear seasonal reproductive pattern, as is seen in their prey (i.e., deer and elk). The usual litter size is 2 to 4 kittens. Females typically produce their first litter at 2 years of age and care for their young until the kittens are 12 to 20 months old. Young mountain lions are quite large at 1 year of age, and soon leave their mothers' care to establish their own home ranges.

Breeding history and research on the distribution of home ranges show that mountain lion populations are composed of resident adults, dependent young, and dispersing, or transient, lions. Replacement or displacement of mountain lions into previously occupied home ranges and the dispersion into new areas are part of the natural history of these animals. However, this dispersion into new and sometimes sub-optimal areas on the fringe of urban areas or other areas of high human activity is what often puts mountain lions in conflict with humans.

The life of a predator is a tough one. The life span of a mountain lion in the wild is typically less than 10 years, although older animals have been reported. In captivity, mountain lions have been known to live as long as 20 years. Survival of mountain lions is variable and is influenced by a variety of mortality factors. Natural mortality factors include age, disease, injury, and mountain lions that kill each other. This aggressive behavior can be a major cause of mortality in some mountain lion populations. Other mortality factors include hunting and the killing of mountain lions that have attacked or killed livestock. Near the urban fringe, vehicular deaths can also take a large toll on mountain lion populations.

WHERE DO MOUNTAIN LIONS LIVE?

Although mountain lions are highly evolved predators, they are considered generalists in the sense that they occur over an impressive variety of habitats throughout North, Central, and South America.

From the rain forests of British Columbia to the southwestern deserts, as well as above timberline in the Andes, they have one of the broadest geographic distributions of any land mammal in the western hemisphere.

The distribution of mountain lions in North America and Canada follows the distribution of prey species—primarily deer, elk, and bighorn sheep in coastal, interior, and desert mountains. Mountain lions require suitable vegetative cover and topographic ruggedness for stalking and ambushing prey. Ambushes can occur in the relatively open habitats of mountains, hills, and drainages, but only if the terrain provides enough cover for mountain lions to approach prey. Similarly, mountain lions can attack in less rugged areas, such as the lower elevations of hills and mountains and in river bottoms that provide suitable vegetative cover.

Historically, mountain lions were spread throughout most of North America, but today they are limited to the western United States and Canada.

MOUNTAIN LION COUNTRY

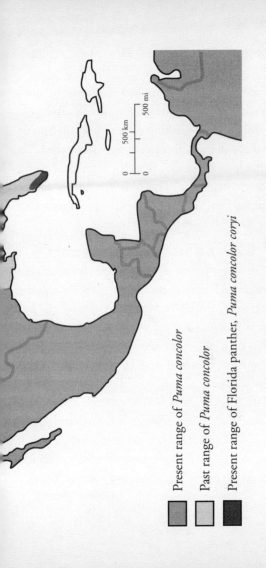

Present range of *Puma concolor*

Past range of *Puma concolor*

Present range of Florida panther, *Puma concolor coryi*

The early settlement of the East included a dramatic conversion of habitat to agricultural and urban uses, with unregulated hunting of both prey and predator. Although their historical prey, white-tailed deer, have made an impressive recovery in the East, mountain lions have not. The only remaining eastern mountain lion, the Florida panther, is endangered. Fewer than 50 remain in the state.

WHAT DO MOUNTAIN LIONS EAT?

In North America, deer are mountain lions' primary prey, although they also subsist seasonally on other ungulates (hoofed mammals) such as elk and bighorn sheep. Mountain lions are opportunists, preying on a wide variety of alternate or secondary prey, including small and large wild mammals, domestic livestock, and pets. Wild mammals common in the mountain lion diet include mule deer, white-tailed deer, elk, bighorn sheep, peccaries, wild pigs, coyotes, bobcats, foxes, raccoons, beavers, porcupines, opossums, hares and rabbits, skunks, marmots, ground squirrels, and smaller rodents.

Domestic or exotic animals killed by mountain lions are equally diverse, and include cattle, sheep, goats, pigs, horses, ostriches, emus, llamas, dogs (all breeds and sizes), and cats.

Mountain lions are solitary hunters, and reports of lions killing elk, cattle (500–800 pounds), and llamas (350 pounds) are a testament to their predatory abilities. Although mountain lions do prey on smaller animals, it is believed that the energy requirements of females with dependent young require the presence of larger "deer-sized" prey. This is certainly reflected in the lions' geographic distribution. Domestic sheep, young cattle, and goats, also "deer-sized," are the predominant livestock killed by mountain lions and may provide a very important alternate prey in many areas. Ranchers have long known the appeal of their livestock to mountain lions.

HOW OFTEN DO MOUNTAIN LIONS FEED?

There are no absolute rules here. Feeding rates vary with prey size and availability, energy needs (i.e., size, dependent young) of the mountain lion, and climate. A mountain lion may kill a deer as often as every other day or as infrequently as every other week. Estimating kill rates is very difficult and requires monitoring (using radio telemetry) sequential kills by individual mountain lions. In theory, deer kill rates should be highest when prey are most vulnerable and energy demands of mountain lions are highest. An example would be a female lion with dependent young feeding on deer concentrated on winter range. But many other factors—especially other predators—impact the mountain lion's kill rate. Grizzly bears and wolves may displace mountain lions from their kills, and thus force them to hunt again. Black bears are also known to feed secondarily on mountain lion kills and so may also serve to increase the mountain lion's kill rate.

Mountain lions may feed on kills for periods ranging from 1 night to as long as 3 weeks depending on the availability and size of the prey, disturbance by secondary predators such as bears, wolves, and coyotes, and the rate of spoilage. In colder climates, mountain lions may feed on an elk for over two weeks. In the deserts of southeastern California, an adult mountain lion was recorded feeding on a large bighorn sheep ram for approximately a week.

Kill rates are often used to try to describe the potential impact that mountain lions have on prey populations. But whether looking at collective kill rates or estimates of an individual lion's kill rate, the numbers give us only crude approximations that vary widely, both over time and between populations. While it is recognized that mountain lions can be a significant mortality factor for prey populations, it has been traditionally assumed that predators do not control the numbers of prey, but rather may influence the magnitude of response of prey numbers to changes in the environment (i.e., forage conditions). Depressed prey numbers make for an exception to this rule. Recent studies show, for example, that predation may be preventing the recovery of threatened bighorn sheep populations in California. In this circumstance, the mountain lions feed primarily on deer and hunt the bighorn sheep seasonally. Since the presence of the deer population frees the mountain lions from having to depend on their predation of bighorn sheep for survival, the number of lions is not tied to the number of bighorn sheep as it would be if the sheep were the lions' primary prey. Thus a stable to increasing population of lions hunts a continually dwindling population of bighorn sheep. Similarly, under circumstances where other types of alternate prey are readily available, such as domestic animals or wild pigs, predation may greatly influence numbers of threatened native wildlife populations.

HOW DO MOUNTAIN LIONS KILL AN ANIMAL?

A mountain lion's attack is characteristic of that of other solitary cat predators. This mode of attack is one of stalk and ambush, requiring tremendous stealth, strength, keen sight and hearing, speed, and cover. During attack, a mountain lion positions its body close to the ground and moves silently toward the prey. The attack ends in a short burst of speed that allows the lion to grasp the prey by the back of the neck. The mountain lion extends its claws to grab and hold the prey. Using its canines to bite the throat, a mountain lion will kill most medium to large prey by suffocation. I've examined several carcasses of bighorn sheep and desert mule deer in Arizona where the fatal bites were delivered to the throat and the animals died by suffocation. Fatal bites to the neck that separate the vertebrae, or "break" the neck, may occur on smaller prey.

Mountain lions are capable of killing prey much larger than themselves. The mountain lion's hunting style optimizes its chances of encountering and effectively killing prey. Hunting strategy likely varies with the distribution, size, and activity of the prey. But because mountain lions are extremely difficult to study, little has been documented about the exact details of their hunting strategy. However, for decades, animal damage control specialists and biologists have been able to "piece together" the scenarios under which prey were killed. Additionally, biologists using radio telemetry can now track mountain lions to examine their routes and investigate sequential kills. In Idaho, Dr. John Seidensticker noted that a hunting mountain lion traverses areas with suitable cover to "optimize" encounters with wintering deer and elk. In California, Dr. Paul Beier describes a less active hunting style. He observed hunting mountain lions "stalking and sitting in ambush" and then moving to another area. They repeated this pattern several times during one night.

After killing larger prey, such as deer or bighorn sheep, mountain lions usually first open the body cavity under the ribs, remove and consume the vital organs (i.e., heart, and liver) and leave a gut pile. Next they eat the thigh muscles. The entire carcass may eventually be consumed, depending on how many days the lion returns to feed. The carcass is usually dragged under a bush or tree (if available), and further concealed by scraping soil, sticks, and leaf litter over the kill. The mountain lion may return to feed for several nights.

Mountain lions are most active during the night and at dawn/dusk. Their large eyes and their ability to open (dilate) the pupils very wide for enhanced light gathering give them excellent night vision. However, mountain lion hunting activity should be expected to reflect the activity of their prey. For example, when prey are more active during the day, a mountain lion's activity pattern would be expected to adjust accordingly.

HOW MANY MOUNTAIN LIONS ARE THERE?

Estimated cougar population is greater than 4,000, based solely on "regional intuition."
—KNUT ATKINSON, BRITISH COLUMBIA, CANADA, 1996 MOUNTAIN LION WORKSHOP

"How many are there?" is the question most frequently asked about mountain lions. It is also one of the most difficult questions to answer. Knut Atkinson's answer of more than 4,000 mountain lions in British Columbia based on "regional intuition" is both imprecise and admirably honest. Knowing "how many" is the holy grail to those who study wildlife populations. Estimating numbers of animals is a complex science that sets into play a multitude of sampling methods always being redesigned to try to optimize our guess. Even the best methods and efforts yield population estimates that are quite variable, and estimates for large geographic areas, for example a state, will always be imprecise. Interestingly, 4,000 mountain lions in British Columbia seems high to some individuals (like us wildlife biologists), yet to someone living in a metropolitan area of 3.5 million people, the estimate may seem precariously (or reassuringly) low. It is all a matter of scale and perspective, with the more important question being "how are the numbers changing over time?"

At the 1996 Fifth Mountain Lion Workshop in San Diego, California, representatives from western states and provinces reported their best assessment of the population status of mountain lions in their respective regions. Although almost all of the 12 western states, 1 eastern (Florida), and 2 Canadian provinces (British Columbia and Alberta) reported stable to increasing populations of mountain lions, their population estimates could more appropriately be described as "educated guesses" based on very simplistic models. In fact, 4 states including Montana, New Mexico, Texas, and Wyoming reported that they didn't have enough information to provide a statewide population estimate. Why is this? Simple: 1) population estimates for a low density, solitary, secretive animal are extremely difficult to obtain; and 2) expanding local estimates has limited value, as there is little usefulness in a "statewide" population of mountain lions—management and conservation efforts are usually directed at more regional levels. The only precise population estimate may be from Florida, simply because fewer than 50 panthers remain, and they are monitored as part of a substantial conservation effort.

Mountain lions do not recognize provincial boundaries, state lines, or city limits. Their numbers vary regionally with the availability of suitable habitat and prey. It is more interesting and of greater consequence to know how populations are changing at a more localized level. Most states have a variety of "indices" of mountain lion activity, such as annual hunting harvest, sightings, local studies, depredation activity (livestock or pets killed), track surveys, past management practices (i.e., bounty programs), and status of prey populations, on which they base their population-trend speculations. Based on these indices, most wildlife agencies believe that mountain lion populations are stable and/or increasing. Mountain lion populations are believed to have rebounded from the days of bounty hunting and other unrestricted hunting.

It may be more intuitive to consider densities of adult mountain lions, as determined from radio telemetry studies. Mountain lion densities have been measured to vary from 0.5 to 4 adults per 40 square miles (100 square kilometers) in North America. As with home range size, densities may vary dramatically between habitats and seasons based upon the distribution and density of prey. For example, higher densities of mountain lions are reported where deer concentrate seasonally on winter ranges. As a general rule, mountain lion numbers are higher in areas with higher densities of prey and suitable cover.

4

Mountain Lion Identification and Field Sign

Deadly and successful in dealing with their natural prey, the pumas in relation to man are singularly shy, skulking, elusive creatures with marvelous facility for keeping out of sight.
—Edward A. Goldman, 1946

DO MOUNTAIN LIONS LIVE IN YOUR AREA?

Most people do not realize how elusive mountain lions are. Do you simply see them if they are nearby? Can you easily observe and take pictures of them? The answer to both questions is "no." Even wildlife researchers who intensively monitor these animals with radio telemetry rarely see them. Mountain lions typically are caught for these projects using snares or dogs, tranquilized, equipped with a radio transmitting collar, released, and rarely seen again unless recaptured. It is often essential to monitor these animals from aircraft because of the great distances they can travel.

If we can see mountain lions only very rarely, how do we know if they might be nearby? The best way to tell is to look for signs of deer. Prey abundance is the best indicator of the potential presence of lions. "So, if I don't see deer, then that means there are no mountain lions, right?" Not always, although the presence of mountain lions is certainly less likely. Mountain lions feed on a wide variety of wild and domestic animals. Habitat that provides adequate topography and cover is also a good secondary indicator. For example, mountain lions are unlikely to occur in flat, open valleys, grasslands, mesas, or areas opened up by human activity. Remember though, with adaptive animals like mountain lions, there are no certain rules.

How else might you know if mountain lions are nearby? You can try "reading sign" or detecting the past presence of a mountain lion. Reading sign requires knowing what to look for and careful attention to detail. Part of the pleasure of being in the outdoors is learning to open your senses to the signs all around you. Experienced trackers are students of this outdoor discipline.

Telling someone how to read sign is like telling someone how to play the piano. The only way to learn is to be shown and to practice.—HARLEY SHAW, 1983

Signs to look for include tracks, a concealed kill, drag marks, a gut pile, "scrapes" (also called scratches), and scat (feces piles). To correctly identify mountain lion tracks, *both* size and shape must be considered. Tracks can be characterized by the 4 toe pads and rear heel pad from each foot. Adult mountain lion paws are quite large, and only the prints of large domestic dogs and Canadian lynx, and the hind prints of wolves, fit within a similar range of sizes (about 3.5 inches wide and 3.5 inches long) and shapes. If you come across tracks that show distinct claw marks, the tracks are most likely made by a dog or (perhaps) a wolf. Mountain lion claws are ordinarily retracted when walking, and tracks almost never show signs of nail marks. Although some trackers report seeing claw marks in mountain lion tracks, they report these to be very narrow, rather than blunt like those of a dog. Dog tracks can be highly variable, and can resemble mountain lion tracks. Depending on soil compactness and grooming, dog tracks may not clearly show claws. Lynx tracks rarely show a distinct heel pad because of the dense fur which covers their feet. Even black bear tracks can be misidentified as mountain lion tracks. However, a good bear print will show 5 toe pads, claw marks, and a much larger heel pad.

Mountain lion track   **Bobcat track**

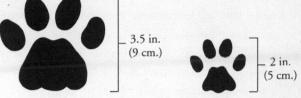

3.5 in.
(9 cm.)

2 in.
(5 cm.)

Feline tracks (forepaw illustrated).
Claws seldom show. Generally circular in shape.

Wolf track   **Dog track**

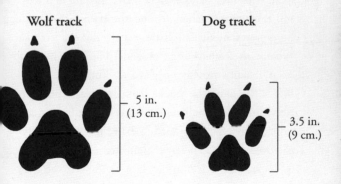

5 in.
(13 cm.)

3.5 in.
(9 cm.)

Canine tracks (forepaw illustrated).
Claws usually show. Length is generally greater than width.

ALL MEASUREMENTS ARE APPROXIMATE.

If you see a track, take your time and look around for a good print. Experts recognize that *shape* is the best key to correctly identifying a mountain lion track. The heel pad in a mountain lion track is triangular in shape, distinctly three-lobed (similarly sized lobes) at the rear, and concave or sometimes flat (never rounded/pointed) at the front. Overall, mountain lion tracks can be described as asymmetrical, meaning you can tell left from right and front from rear. Dogs and wolves move around at a trot; soil is often disturbed around the track. Mountain lions generally disturb little soil around their tracks because they are more careful and deliberate in their steps, usually moving only at a walking pace. When this is the case, the tracks from the rear feet often step into (or immediately in front of) the front track on the same side. So examine the tracks carefully; the front heel pad is larger than the rear. If the track is shaped like a mountain lion track, but the heel pad is less than 1.5 inches (3.8 centimeters) wide, it may be either a mountain lion kitten, bobcat, or domestic cat. In rare circumstances, mountain lion kitten tracks may be observed, though these tracks will usually be accompanied by those of an adult. For those of you interested in learning more about the tracks and sign of a variety of animals, I recommend *A Field Guide to Mammal Tracking in Western America* by James Halfpenny (Boulder, Colorado: Johnson Books, 1986).

Other "sign" of mountain lions—including kills, scrapes, and feces (scat)—are rarely observed and are not easily identified without training. For the novice, scrapes and feces should not be considered evidence on their own; so also look for tracks. Scrapes are small piles of leaves, soil, or ground litter that measure about 6 to 18 inches (15 to 45 centimeters) in length and are slightly narrower in width. Scrapes are not readily or frequently observed unless one is tracking lions, and are not usually found on trails, but off to the side. Mountain lion scrapes are generally made by male lions and are believed to serve as communication between mountain lions to advertise presence and delimit home range. Mountain lions often urinate or defecate in or near these piles. Feces are also infrequently observed because mountain lions often bury them (sometimes only lightly). The size and shape of the stool is variable, but is generally several inches long, 1 to 1.5 inches in diameter, and with deep segmentation. Stools produced by other predators such as coyotes, bobcats, Canadian lynxes, and wolves can be similar, and are sometimes mistaken for mountain lion scat. Animals killed by mountain lions, if found, can sometimes be distinguished from those killed by bears, wolves and dogs. For more on this, turn to Chapter 11.

HAVE YOU HEARD A MOUNTAIN LION?

Probably not. Even if you hear one of their characteristic vocalizations, the sounds are not singular enough to provide certain identification unless you are very experienced. Wilderness trackers and rural trail hikers describe an incredible variety of mountain lion calls. But alas, mountain lions are best characterized by their silence and do not announce their presence. Interestingly, I get a lot of phone calls regarding "screams" or "screeches" heard that the callers are sure indicate that a mountain lion has taken up residence on their property. Most of these "screams" have been some of the best imitations of the sounds made by barn owls, coyotes, and foxes I've ever heard.

Although only rarely vocal, mountain lions make a variety of unusual sounds. The characteristic "cry" heard on episodes of *Lassie* or Walt Disney specials is not often heard. In fact, most sounds that mountain lions make are relatively quiet and are intended for close communication. These sounds include soft whistle-type mews, purring, and meow-like calls. Louder growls and cries resembling, but deeper than, those of domestic cats are also made as accompaniment to mating or fighting. I have heard mountain lions vocalize in captive situations and have heard a variety of louder vocalizations on tapes provided to me by colleagues. Unfortunately, in the wild, I have not heard anything that I could confidently identify as a sound made by a mountain lion.

HAVE YOU SEEN A MOUNTAIN LION?

Most people would think that they could not possibly mistake a mountain lion if they spotted one in the wild. Yet many sightings are not accurate. All too often a follow-up to a reported sighting turns out to be a coyote, bobcat, yellow Labrador retriever, or domestic cat. Even mountain lions reported to be seen dead on the roadside are often coyotes, domestic dogs, or bobcats. Just recently a motorist called me on a cellular phone to report a dead mountain lion on the side of a major interstate highway in suburban south Sacramento. The caller was very excited, and when I asked him to describe what he saw, he responded rather indignantly, "I know what a mountain lion looks like!" It turned out to be a dead coyote.

Many "sightings" are made with the help of a pair of glaring headlights, while traveling. Although a sense of scale or size is not very good under such situations, the "gestalt" or look of a mountain lion is distinct if you consider the tail and general body shape. Mountain lion tails are very long and heavily furred, almost as long as the body, or 40 percent of total length. The tail usually hangs low; only rarely is it positioned high. The head, relative to the size and length of the body, appears small and round (short muzzle), and a mountain lion's coloring is distinctly plain. These simple visual features should be enough to identify an adult mountain lion. Reflective eye-shine is greenish gold. Note that this color does not provide certain identification, as it is similar to that found in the eyes of the coyote, bobcat, and other large mammals.

Adult males generally weigh between 100 and 160 pounds (45 to 73 kilograms), and are 78 to 91 inches (6.5 to 7.6 feet, or 198 to 231 centimeters) long from nose to tail. Exceptionally large males weighing more than 200 pounds are periodically reported. Adult females weigh between 75 and 105 pounds (34 to 48 kilograms), and are 69 to 80 inches

(5.8 to 6.7 feet, or 175 to 203 centimeters) long. Although males are larger than females, the sexes cannot be distinguished easily in the field, as the testes of males are not visibly obvious. Sizes of mountain lions vary according to geography, with animals of larger size found at more northern latitudes.

Mountain lions have proportionately longer hind legs than any other member of the cat family, and this gives them a slightly downward appearing stance. The stance is adapted for jumping and short bursts of speed for ambushing prey. The front legs and shoulder region are very strong and muscular. The paws are large. In fact, the front paws are slightly larger than those in the rear. In proportion to the body, the head appears small; yet like other cats, the head is broad and muscular with a short muzzle capable of delivering a powerful bite.

The color of adult mountain lions varies from gray-brown to red-brown, but the most common shade is tawny (yellowish). Mountain lions are further distinguished by dark markings at the end of the tail, the back sides of the ears, and in the whiskers area (sides of the snout). These animals are white or a light color underneath the body, on the front/inside of the ears, and at the front of the mouth area. Until approximately 8 months of age, young lions have distinct dark spots on their fur. At 1 to $1^1/_2$ years of age, some spotting may still be visible on the hindquarters. Mountain lions are born with light blue eyes which gradually change to the distinct yellowish-brown of adults by 1 to $1^1/_2$ years of age, although sometimes this change happens much sooner.

There is no easy way to estimate the age of a mountain lion in the field. Estimation of size and weight, even by experienced observers, is unreliable. Long-time mountain lion trackers and researchers can generally recognize younger lions by the relatively narrower head and proportionately larger eyes and ears. But you can best age mountain lions by examining their teeth, especially looking at tooth replacement, eruption patterns, and wear. Of course,

TABLE 2. *Summary of adult mountain lion physical features.*

Feature	Description
Coloration (body)	Distinctly plain gray to yellowish to red-brown above, whitish underneath, black-tipped tail, black behind ears and in whisker area on muzzle. Spotting on fur usually indicates bobcat or lynx, which noticeably lack a long tail.
Coloration (tail)	Same color as body with black tip.
Tail Length	Long and thick, almost equal to body length, or 40% of total length. Tail is 2.5 to 3.5 feet long.
Total Length	Tail and body 6 to 8 feet long, body 3.5 to 4.5 feet long.
Weight	75 to 160 pounds.
Head Size/Shape	Small relative to body, and round (short muzzle).

Mountain lion

this requires that you be "up close and personal" with an animal that is either dead or tranquilized. If you ever find yourself in such a situation, you could take a look at the mountain lion's 3 distinct tooth types: 1) front incisors for grasping and tearing meat; 2) elongated canines for holding and killing prey; and 3) sharp molars and premolars for shearing meat prior to swallowing. The pattern of eruption of the molars and premolars, and the wear of the incisors and canines, provide the clues to a mountain lion's age.

Bobcat

To identify a bobcat, note the short tail, distinct dark spotting or banding on legs, some spotting on body, long hair in cheek region, darker long hair pointing off the tops of the ears (sometimes hard to see), and smaller size.

Mountain Lion Fact and Fiction

1. Mountain lions are commonly seen, if present. *False*

Mountain lions are masters of stealth and, as a rule, are rarely seen. Also, the dawn/dusk and night activity peaks of mountain lions do not coincide with human activity. Due to the rarity of observation, the fact that a mountain lion is repeatedly seen in an area is a criterion used by wildlife agencies to evaluate an animal that may be a public safety concern.

2. Mountain lions are vocal and can be commonly heard, if present. *False*

Mountain lions are better known for their silence. Vocalizations are heard so rarely that it is more likely

that you are hearing some other animal. Most vocalizations by mountain lions are "close range"
sounds, intended to communicate with dependent
young, and you are very unlikely to hear any of this
intimate chatter. Although lions may vocalize loudly
during mating or when fighting, even these sounds
are rarely heard. Mountain lions do not usually
vocalize when approaching prey or humans.

3. Mountain lions roam only in the wilderness.

False

It is easy to imagine that mountain lions occupy
only remote, "undisturbed" wildernesses. This seems
natural: we rarely see mountain lions, and they
appear to have a natural aversion to humans. Yet
mountain lions commonly wander in areas with high
levels of human activity. I recall discussing the distribution of mountain lions with a Fish and Game
biologist who monitored the first radio-collared
mountain lions in California in the early 1970s.
This was the first time this technology was used to

monitor mountain lions, and small airplanes were equipped with receivers to find and document the animals' movements. The biologist was most impressed that "the cougars were commonly around campgrounds with people." He added, "I was amazed that nobody saw or reported them. We did not expect this." Mountain lions are also reported in the valley area of Yosemite National Park during some of the highest periods of human recreation! This phenomenon is also seen in other areas of California, where human development has encroached on mountain lion habitat. In these areas, habitat loss and fragmentation, not simply human activity, will ultimately determine the fate of both mountain lions and deer.

4. Mountain lions are solitary.   *True*

Yes, mountain lions are solitary animals. However, males pair with females during brief and intense mating periods. During this time, you might hear loud vocalizations. These mating periods typically last less than a couple of days. The males do not participate in rearing young. Females will care vigilantly for young until 1 to 1½ years of age. The kittens can be quite large prior to leaving the adult female and they may travel together as a group.

5. Mountain lions have strict, non-overlapping territories. *False*

Mountain lion territories vary over time and place. Because their boundaries are somewhat fluid, it is more appropriate to refer to these areas as home ranges. Individual mountain lions communicate using sense of smell and also visually by scrapes, feces, and urine to advertise their presence in an area. As a general rule, male mountain lion home ranges overlap those of several females, but rarely those of other males. Females are more tolerant of each other than are males, and their home ranges may overlap considerably in some situations, but they avoid meeting one another.

6. Mountain lions den in caves. *True and false*

Mountain lions are somewhat indiscriminate about where they give birth and raise their young. More often than not, they simply select an area of dense underbrush, an overhang of tree roots or logs, earthen or rock caves, or even the space under old, deserted buildings. The areas they choose must offer thermal protection and provide cover for their young. Within 3-4 months, the young are old enough to be relatively mobile, and they abandon these sites.

7. Mountain lion populations are increasing
   rapidly. *True and false*

During the past 30 years, both numbers and distribution of mountain lions have undoubtedly increased in western North America, since the elimination of bounty hunting and other unregulated hunting. This increase has been coincident with increasing human populations and contributes to the perception that mountain lion populations are becoming overabundant in many regions. Western North America is a mosaic of different habitats, prey densities, and human impacts that vary from region to region, and predator populations should be expected to vary accordingly.

8. Regulated hunting has threatened mountain lion populations. *False*

Hunting seems to have little or no effect. Western states continue today to regulate hunting, and yet report stable-to-increasing populations. California, with no hunting program since 1972, reports similar population trends. Regulated hunting has not been shown to threaten the viability of regional mountain lion populations.

9. Mountain lions are endangered.

Mostly not true

Mountain lion populations have been reported to be stable to increasing during the past 30 years in western North America. Although populations occur in relatively low densities, they are common within deer, bighorn sheep, and elk habitat. Future survival of mountain lions, as well as their prey, will be jeopardized in areas where habitat is lost to human development. Mountain lions are no longer found in the eastern United States, and the Florida panther (a subspecies) is federally listed as endangered.

10. Mountain lions are aggressive toward people. *Mostly not true*

Ordinarily, this animal is very shy and wary of humans. Attacks on people are extremely rare. For example, in the western United States millions of people recreate in mountain lion habitat every year. And wildlife agencies receive hundreds of reports from hikers, hunters, mountain bikers, trail runners, and equestrians about mountain lion incidents or "encounters." Yet only a few of these encounters have resulted in physical contact of any kind. Mountain lions are also curious animals, and many people in the outdoors report being followed or approached, only to have the animal leave without incident. Makes me wonder how many times this has happened without my knowing it!

Tragically though, mountain lions have attacked a few people. And these uncharacteristic occurrences have prompted wildlife agencies to define safety policies and educate the public about the possible risks of living and playing in mountain lion country.

11. Lions feed only on fresh kills. *True and false*

Mountain lions generally feed only on animals that they have killed. Depending on a variety of circumstances, mountain lions may feed on a carcass for days and weeks—way past "fresh." They may also feed on carrion, but this is not generally the case. When prey is abundant, mountain lions sometimes consume only certain vital organs before moving on.

12. Mountain lions are attracted to and feed on pet food or garbage. *False*

This is a common misconception. If a mountain

lion is seen around pet food, believe me, it is looking for something else.

13. Mountain lions are afraid of dogs.
True and false

Mountain lions can be chased and "treed" by one or more dogs. These are situations when the dogs have the advantage, because they are barking *after* the mountain lion. Conversely, a mountain lion often has the advantage of stealth, and hunting mountain lions kill and eat all sizes and breeds of dogs. Our records in the western United States show that all dogs—from rottweilers to dachshunds—are fair game.

Safe Travel in Mountain Lion Country: How to Handle an Encounter

WHERE AM I, AND
WHAT WILDLIFE ARE NEARBY?

Any outdoor adventure requires preparation. You spend time planning your route and packing gear, water, and food. And, hopefully, you think about safety and quickly check on the weather, re-stock your first-aid kit, and let family and friends know of your route and anticipated time of return. Learning about the wildlife you can expect to encounter is also an important part of outdoor fun and safety.

The most important safety element for recreation in mountain lion habitat is simply recognizing potential mountain lion habitat. But how do you know if you are in mountain lion country? Well, there are several clues, some of which I have discussed already. Consider the distribution of deer, the primary prey of mountain lions in North America. For those experienced in the outdoors, such as hunters, deer are relatively easy to see if they are present. However, if you are not experienced at observing deer, or at recognizing their tracks or feces, this may not be a helpful clue. In this case, talk to locals, park rangers, or state wildlife biologists. Fish and wildlife agencies usually have good information about deer distribution from population surveys and hunting results.

Deer tracks can be found easily on dirt roads and trails. The illustration on page 75 shows the relative dimensions of deer tracks, which average about 3 inches in length. Elk tracks are similar, but are larger and average about 4 to 4.5 inches (10 to

Deer scat

Deer track

12 centimeters) long. Note that deer tracks can be confused with those of other hoofed mammals (and prey), such as domestic sheep, goats, and pigs. Seek the advice of someone knowledgeable, or refer to a book on animal tracks.

An important feature of mountain lion habitat is relative openness of terrain. Mountain lions do not usually roam flat and "open" areas like the central valley of California, the creosote desert flats of southwestern states, or the grassland/sage pronghorn antelope ranges of the western states. However, they might be found along rivers running through these areas.

SAFETY GUIDELINES FOR TRAVELING IN MOUNTAIN LION COUNTRY

Is it as simple as just staying out of mountain lion country? Of course not. If you did, there would be few places left to explore. Be aware of the wildlife around you, respect them, be prepared, and enjoy. Follow these safety tips:

1. Travel with a friend or group.
2. Keep small children close.
3. Do not let pets run unleashed.
4. Try to minimize your recreation during dawn and dusk—the times mountain lions are most active.
5. Carry a weapon or deterrent device (see page 82) within quick reach—like in your fanny pack. (Remember that firearms may be illegal in many recreation areas.) Most attack victims have little or no warning.
6. Respect park warning signs or notices of mountain lion activity.
7. Know how to behave if you encounter a mountain lion.

WHAT TO DO IF YOU ENCOUNTER
A MOUNTAIN LION—
YOUR BEHAVIOR IS IMPORTANT

In the vast majority of mountain lion encounters, these animals exhibit avoidance, indifference, or curiosity that never results in human injury. But it is natural to be alarmed if you have an encounter of any kind. Try to keep your cool and consider the following:

1. Recognize threatening mountain lion behavior. There are a few cues that may help you gauge the risk of attack. If a mountain lion is more than 50 yards away, changes positions, directs attention toward people, and exhibits following behavior, it may be only curious. This circumstance represents only a slight risk for adults, but a more serious risk to unaccompanied children. At this point, you should move away, while keeping the animal in your peripheral vision. Also, take out a deterrent device or look for rocks, sticks, or something to use as a weapon, just in case.

For distances of *less than 50 yards,* where the animal is staring intensely and hiding, it may be assessing the chances of a successful attack. If *intense staring and hiding continue, accompanied by crouching and creeping,* the risk of attack may be substantial.

2. Do not approach a mountain lion; give the animal the opportunity to move on. Slowly back away, but maintain eye contact if close. Mountain lions are not known to attack humans to defend young or a kill, but they have been reported to "charge" in rare instances and may want to stay in the area. Best choose another route or time to adventure through the area.

3. Do not run from a mountain lion. Running may stimulate a predatory response.

4. If you encounter a mountain lion, be vocal and talk or yell loudly and regularly. Try not to panic: shout in a way that others in the area may understand to make them aware of the situation.

5. Maintain eye contact. Eye contact presents a challenge to the mountain lion, showing that

Hiker "looking big"

you are aware of its presence. Eye contact also helps you know where it is. However, if the behavior of the mountain lion is not threatening (if it is, for example, grooming or periodically looking away), maintain visual contact through your peripheral vision and move away.

6. Appear larger than you are. Raise your arms above your head and make steady waving

motions. Raise your jacket or another object above your head. Do not bend over as this will make you appear smaller and more "prey-like."

7. If you are with small children, pick them up. First bring children close to you, maintain eye contact with the mountain lion, and pull the children up without bending over. Band together, if you are with other children or adults.

8. Be prepared to defend yourself and fight back, if attacked. Try to remain standing. Do not feign death. Pick up a branch or rock, pull out a knife, pepper spray, or other deterrent device. Remember, everything is a potential weapon, and individuals have fended off mountain lions with blows from rocks, tree limbs, and even cameras.

9. Defend your friends or children, but not your pet. In past attacks on children, adults have successfully stopped attacks. However, such cases are very dangerous and risky, and I do not recommend physically defending a pet.

10. Respect any warning signs posted by agencies. It may not be a good time for outdoor adventuring.

11. Teach others in your group how to behave. One person or child who starts running could precipitate an attack.

12. If you have an encounter with a mountain lion, record your location and the details of the encounter, and notify the nearest park official, land owner, or other appropriate agency. The land management agency (federal, state, or county) may want to visit the site and, if appropriate, post education/warning signs. Fish and wildlife agencies should also be notified because they record and track such encounters. Remember, agencies need accurate information regarding your encounter. However, given the frequency of mountain lion sightings, many, including yours, may not be followed up on unless the animal exhibited unusually bold behavior. Remember, just because you see a mountain lion

does not mean the animal is a threat to your safety. These agencies expect people to see mountain lions. You should not expect authorities to kill a curious mountain lion.

If physical injury occurs, it is important to leave the area and not disturb the site of attack. Mountain lions that have attacked people must be killed, and an undisturbed site is critical for effectively locating the dangerous mountain lion.

ARE THERE ANY EFFECTIVE DETERRENTS?

The effectiveness of any deterrent depends on many factors. For example, pepper spray (capsaicin-based) may be useful for incidents where a mountain lion is observed nearby and is approaching. It is uncertain, however, how effective the spray may be once an attack has occurred. It is difficult to advocate a particular device, as circumstances and expertise vary dramatically from person to person. Potential weapons and deterrent devices include: knives, walking sticks, pepper spray, and firearms. If you choose to carry a deterrent device, be sure you not only know how to use it but are also confident and comfortable with it *before* you venture into mountain lion country. In the event of an attack, everything is a potential weapon: people have fought off lions with nothing more than rocks and sticks. (Remember that firearms may be illegal in many recreation areas.)

Safety Tips for Trail Runners, Trail Riders, and Mountain Bikers

TRAIL RUNNERS

If you are going to run on trails through mountain lion habitat, run with others! An unleashed pet is not an adequate substitute for a running partner. Tragically, mountain lions have attacked trail runners. A woman runner was killed in California in 1994, and a man was killed in Colorado in 1990. In both cases the runners were alone and unable to successfully defend themselves after the initial attack.

TRAIL RIDERS

Mountain lions have approached individuals on horseback in several states and provinces. In 1996, a family, including a mother and three children, was trail riding on horseback in British Columbia, when a mountain lion suddenly jumped from a bush at the 6-year-old son. The boy was thrown from his horse and was attacked by the mountain lion. The mothr fought off the animal courageously, but she finally was killed by the mountain lion. Surprisingly, this male mountain lion weighed only 65 pounds.

For safety, ride in a group and try to avoid the low-light hours of dawn and dusk. Be alert to any behavioral "cues" that your horse may exhibit. Your horse is likely to smell or see a mountain lion before you do. If a mountain lion appears on the trail, try to keep your horse calm, back away, and leave the area. Do not dismount unless absolutely necessary. In the event that you are thrown from your horse or are forced to dismount, carry some type of deterrent device with you in a fanny pack.

MOUNTAIN BIKERS

Every year numerous cyclists report sightings of mountain lions, and a few of these trailway encounters have necessitated the cyclist's retreat. In 1995, a Southern California cyclist saw a mountain lion quickly approaching. He dismounted and used his bike to shield himself from the cougar. His reactions were appropriate, but they failed. As a last resort, he ran away, slipping down a steep slope. The mountain lion followed and bit him on the head. He reacted by striking the mountain lion in the head with a rock, after which the animal retreated. Like equestrians and trail runners, mountain bikers should always carry some type of deterrent device in a fanny pack.

Protecting Your Property and Family

To meet the growing demand for housing away from less desirable metropolitan centers, developers are quickly converting farmlands, ranchlands, and wildlands into new suburban and sub-rural communities. Many large farms and ranches are being replaced by mini "ranchettes," where homeowners stable a few "hobby" livestock. Although total numbers of livestock in these changing areas may decrease, potential prey (domestic animals) still remain, and resulting conflicts are likely to increase.

If you make that move just beyond the city limits, you will likely find a bit more peace and quiet and a lot of new challenges—like learning about the wildlife that may venture onto your property. Many people who move into the urban fringe are unprepared for the reality that deer, mountain lions, bears, and other critters may also be part of their community. Be advised to take the time to learn about all of your new neighbors, both the 2-legged and 4-legged varieties, and if your home sits in deer country, you'd best bet that you are living among mountain lions. To be on the safe side follow these simple guidelines:

GUIDELINES FOR SAFETY
ON YOUR PROPERTY

1. Be alert to the presence of deer. Deer are known to make seasonal movements; so if you see an increase in deer activity in your area, take extra safety precautions. When they are migratory, deer concentrate during the winter, and mountain lion activity should be expected to be high during that season.

2. Do *not* attract deer or other potential prey

animals, such as raccoons, to your property. Enjoy those that wander in, but do not attract them to your property by providing food or salt licks. Recently in an area where suburban homes border the American River in Sacramento County, California, homeowners set out grain and a salt lick to attract deer to the area behind their home. They enjoyed watching the deer and did not consider the possibility that mountain lions might also live in this river corridor. Unfortunately, one night a neighbor arrived home, heard a noise, and looked over the concrete wall that separated the backyard from the river only to be horrified to observe a mountain lion feeding on a deer that had been baited in. Understandably, the neighbor was concerned—he had a small child who played in the yard. Everyone agreed that this artificial feeding program should be stopped.

3. "Open up" an area around your house that you or your pets can frequent by clearing dense, shrubby vegetation. The perimeter cleared may

vary with topography, but design it to your comfort level. Remember, in areas with dense native vegetation, a cleared perimeter may be advocated by your local forestry or fire fighting agency. In 1994, I received a call from a concerned homeowner in Lake County, California. The homeowner was justifiably concerned because he had a mountain lion on his property that continued to "hang around." I was immediately concerned that this lion might be a public safety problem. When I asked the home-owner if he could see the mountain lion, he said, "No, it's hidden in a bush next to my house feeding on a deer." Although this was a serious situation, this was not a mountain lion that normally would pose an unusual threat to "public safety." This was simply a mountain lion doing what mountain lions do—kill and eat deer. The best solution to this problem was to clear away some of the dense, native vegetation near the home.

4. Landscape your yard with native plants that do
   not attract deer. A useful guide is "Plants That
   Resist Deer" in the *Sunset Western Garden
   Book—40th Anniversary Edition* (Menlo Park,
   California: Sunset Publishing Corporation,
   1995). Your local nursery is also a good resource.
5. If your garden attracts deer, consider building
   deer-proof fencing. Contact your local agri-
   culture or wildlife agency for recommendations.
   Types of fencing include high-tensile wire, elec-
   trified high-tensile wire, and various wire mesh
   fences. Mesh fences should be 6 to 8 feet tall.
   They are relatively easy to construct, are long-
   lasting, and cost $1 to $1.50 per foot. The California Department of Fish and Game has an
   excellent booklet entitled *A Gardener's Guide to
   Preventing Deer Damage,* which diagrams fencing configurations and provides the names of
   fencing manufacturers. (Order from: California Department of Fish and Game, Wildlife
   Management Division—Deer Program, 1416
   Ninth Street, Sacramento, CA 95814.)

6. Keep the play areas of children or pets visible and open to your view from the house. Also, consider fencing open areas to further discourage a mountain lion from entering. Although fencing may not prevent a lion from jumping over, it may be enough of a barrier to make entry much less likely. Remember, mountain lions are ambush predators that rely on stealth and surprise as their strategy. Although I have records of mountain lions jumping fences to quickly acquire a small dog or cat, I am not aware of a mountain lion jumping a fence and threatening people.

7. Install outdoor lighting in areas that pets or your family may frequent at night. I do not advocate lighting your property like a nighttime football game, but rather suggest subtle and necessary lighting in appropriate areas for your and your pets' safety.

8. Do *not* let your pets roam at dawn, dusk, or during the night. Cats and dogs of all breeds have been killed and eaten by mountain lions.

Pet depredation is one of the most rapidly increasing problems.

9. Keep livestock in a secure area at night. Barns or other holding areas that also provide security from coyotes and bobcats are particularly important for small and young livestock.

10. Teach children how to behave if they encounter a mountain lion (see Chapter 6).

11. Tell your neighbors and community if you sight a mountain lion or have any depredation problems.

12. Do not leave out trash or garbage. Garbage may attract other potential prey animals, such as raccoons or opossums. Mountain lions are known to feed on a variety of small mammals that are active at night.

Protecting Your Livestock

Ranchers and mountain lions have a long history of conflict. For the greater part of this century, animal damage control agents and bounty programs mitigated the problem. Although the bounty programs were successful at reducing livestock losses, most of these programs were eliminated by the late 1960s. Today livestock losses are high, and wildlife agencies report approximately 1,000 to 1,500 verified livestock depredation incidents annually in the western United States and Canada. Each "incident" may account for several animals being killed. Depredation problems have increased dramatically in most states during the past 25 years despite the decline in grazed livestock. But mountain lions are not the only culprits. Bears, coyotes, and bobcats take their share of livestock.

Mountain lions kill and eat a wide variety of domestic animals, including sheep, goats, cattle, pigs, llamas, ostriches, emus, horses, donkeys, geese, and chickens. The power and ability of these predators is impressive. In California, a 130-pound male lion was shot after he killed a 350-pound llama. This mountain lion was killed as it was pulling the dead llama over a barbed-wire fence!

The stories depicting mountain lions as infamous and unstoppable cattle killers are the stuff of western folklore. Whether these tales are true or not, mountain lions can have a devastating impact on livestock operations, and they often kill numerous animals in a single night. A mountain lion killing 20 or more domestic sheep in a single night is not uncommon. It is believed that this "surplus killing" occurs in situations where domestic animals are concentrated, and the predator response of the mountain lion may be continually stimulated by the animals running about.

There are no simple solutions to help you prevent your animals from being killed by predators. If possible, livestock should be brought into a barn at night, or at least seasonally, when young animals are present or when mountain lion activity is expected to be high in your area. At a minimum, construct a "coyote-proof" yard by using fencing 5.5 feet tall, with an underground apron of galvanized steel attached to the base and extending to a depth of about 6 inches and outward from the yard 12 to 18 inches (this will prevent predators from digging under the fence). Only by constructing a 10-foot-high fence could you provide adequate protection from mountain lion predation, and this option is not financially feasible for larger livestock operations.

Many depredation problems occur when animals are "pastured" or grazed on rangelands bordering deer and mountain lion habitat. Depredation losses can be minimized by herding the animals into an area that can be better protected at night. Shepherds are used when larger flocks of animals are being trailed to different pastures, and they provide added security. Guard dogs may also provide additional security for smaller herds of animals.

Unfortunately, I have seen too many problems with stray and feral dogs harassing and killing native wildlife in California. Therefore, I am reluctant to recommend dogs as an effective deterrent, unless specialized dogs are appropriately trained and monitored.

A common topic of discussion is the profile of a "livestock killer." Does a mountain lion go "bad" and become a livestock killer? Depredation records from California to Montana indicate that male mountain lions are much more likely to be associated with killing medium-to-large domestic animals, such as sheep, goats and cattle. However, data on the ages of these depredating mountain lions are not conclusive. It appears that younger (or dispersing) mountain lions are frequently associated with these problems. This may simply reflect the fact that there is a proportionately higher number of younger animals in a mountain lion population. Because these animals are opportunistic predators, I do not believe that they necessarily kill livestock out of desperation, but rather, opportunity. Livestock are easy prey. What would you expect a powerful predator to do if it encountered a goat or sheep? Therefore, the predominance of male mountain lions associated with killing livestock may reflect the larger home ranges of male mountain lions and the potentially higher encounter rate. Thus, we should expect more young mountain lions (2 to 3 years old) dispersing into new and often sub-optimal areas, such as areas where livestock often are kept, to be associated with attacks. However, these relations are also affected by the distribution of livestock, and the sex ratio (number of males to females) of the mountain lion population under consideration.

Protecting Your Pets

Not only livestock, but also pets are killed and eaten by mountain lions. In California, pet depredation problems are increasing more dramatically than any other form of depredation. Pets typically live closer to your house, and when they are injured or killed by a mountain lion, the proximity to your family can be cause for great concern. Pet losses are likely under-reported, because when pets disappear, owners often assume that the animal simply ran off. It may be hard to find the carcass of smaller breeds of dogs or cats, because the carcass may be carried farther and easily concealed—or fully consumed.

Report to and seek the advice of a wildlife or animal damage control specialist to diagnose and resolve a potential mountain lion attack on your pet.

Mountain lions have demonstrated that all types of cats and dogs are quite edible, regardless of size or pedigree. Unlike livestock depredations, where male mountain lions are most often the perpetrators, an equal proportion of female and male mountain lions are involved in the killing of pets. The reasons for this are uncertain, but may be because of the smaller body size of pets.

To protect your pets in mountain lion country, bring them into your house or a secure dog run at night, feed them during daylight hours, and do not leave food out at night that may attract prey animals. In areas of higher lion activity, consider installing overhead fencing on a dog run for the most effective protection. But beware: pets have been taken by mountain lions from fenced yards while chained outside, and recently a domestic cat was attacked while sunning on the sill of an open window.

Did a Mountain Lion Kill It? Reporting Mountain Lion Kills

Figuring out how an animal died can be difficult. Preserving tracks and other predator sign is very important. Never disturb the site. And keep in mind that many injuries and deaths of domestic animals are not related to predators. Injuries from barbed-wire fences and deaths from disease, poisons, or other causes can be misdiagnosed as predation. Check with local government wildlife and animal control agencies to help you identify the cause of your animal's injury or death.

In the event that your animal dies, follow up quickly because proper diagnosis becomes more difficult with time, as "secondary" predators (such as bears) come to feed on the carcass. Depending on the weather, carcasses can decay rapidly and make proper diagnosis difficult or impossible. Even after decomposition, blood spots and drag marks may be evident on the ground if the cause of death was predation. However, the type of predator may remain uncertain.

The first step to identifying the cause of death is to determine if your animal was killed by a predator, which may or may not be a mountain lion. Look for signs of a struggle, blood spots on the ground, tracks, drag marks, and other predator sign such as feces. If drag marks are present, continue to look for sign while following the drag path to the kill site. Evidence of blood and external damage on the animal are likely indicators that the animal was killed by a predator. Also, animals killed by a predator usually have their limbs extended, as opposed to being positioned underneath their body, as when they have bedded down. Because blood may not always be visible, examine the head and neck for damage and bleeding, and also skin out this region and look for hemorrhage and tooth-puncture marks.

In the event of an injury to your livestock, look for the injury site by following your animal's pathway (tracks or blood) and look for predator sign and tracks. Also, seek help from wildlife or animal damage control specialists.

After you have determined that death or injury is attributable to a predator, how do you know if the predator was a mountain lion? Did any sign at the kill site provide clues? Mountain lions are very skilled and efficient predators, and their kills are often distinguished by an absence of external damage to the neck and body region of the prey. Mountain lions deliver their fatal bite to the throat and neck region, and puncture wounds from the canines should vary between 1.25 to 2 inches apart (3 to 5 centimeters). Death is usually by suffocation. Claw marks from gripping and restraining the animal may be evident on the head and shoulders. The body cavity of the prey is usually entered from behind the rib cage, and the guts are removed and vital organs eaten. If the lion continues to feed, the muscular thigh region is consumed next. The carcass is usually dragged from the kill site and concealed by covering it with forest litter and sticks. The process of covering the prey dislodges debris in a variable radius around the animal.

Bobcat and lynx kills are similar and may occur with smaller animals such as birds and young sheep or goats. These predators do not usually attack larger animals. Also, bobcats do not dislodge debris from as large a radius when covering prey. This radius for bobcats is usually less than 1.5 feet. Also, bobcat tracks are less than 2 inches in diameter, with a heel pad of usually less than 1.5 inches.

Bears also attack livestock around the neck and head region, but they bite and claw more profoundly at the head, neck, and back. Although both black and grizzly bears may drag their prey, only grizzly bears usually cover it. The muscled flesh of the hind limbs is usually consumed first.

Wolves, coyotes, and dogs similarly pursue and kill prey. These predators characteristically pursue prey over longer distances, and trails of blood may be evident. These animals are less efficient at killing larger prey, and prey killed typically is bitten all over the body (hindquarters, flanks, shoulders, throat, and head). These predators will eat the vital organs and other gut material and thigh muscle. Domestic dogs will often mutilate the prey, but not consume much. Although wolves and coyotes may remove and bury parts from the carcass, they generally do not conceal the entire carcass. The kill is commonly a mess compared with a lion kill.

REPORTING DEPREDATION

Although mountain lions are opportunistic predators, there is a legitimate concern that once a mountain lion has killed livestock, it may attack again. According to current policy, a mountain lion may be killed if there is evidence it killed livestock or pets. The policies and procedures are designed to target the offending animal, and you should report attacks immediately.

Wildlife agencies vary in their policies and procedures for reporting, verifying, and permitting mountain lions to be killed. In California, wildlife protection personnel (game wardens) are required to verify that your property damage (injured or dead livestock or pet) is attributable to a mountain lion. On verification, they will issue a permit to kill the offending mountain lion under strict pursuit conditions. These pursuit conditions are set as a means to best assure targeting "the" mountain lion that caused your property damage. The permit expires in 10 days. Areas that have high mountain lion activity may also have county and/or federal animal control services that will help diagnose a kill, and also pursue the mountain lion.

Since the support and regulations regarding mountain lion problems with livestock and pets vary among different states and provinces, it is important to contact your local fish and game office to find out the resources and procedures for your area. Most state agencies assign both biologists and game wardens to areas throughout the state. They are part of a community that can help you understand the presence and activity of mountain lions in your area.

A Conservation Dilemma

Mountain lions are indeed back. The question is: Can we make room for them? —MAURICE HORNOCKER, NATIONAL GEOGRAPHIC, 1992

I first encountered a mountain lion in southwestern Arizona while I was tracking radio-collared desert bighorn sheep and mule deer. My job required constant "glassing" of the open desert mountains to locate and, hopefully, not disturb our radio-collared animals. Although I had been working intensely in the field for three and a half years, I had only seen scat, tracks, and a few mountain lion kills. I was always amazed that I would regularly see mountain lion sign, but never a mountain lion. Then it happened—the mortality sensor on a radio-collared desert bighorn ram in the Harquahala Mountains signaled. While locating the dead animal in a canyon, I flushed out a mountain lion. It looked at me briefly—very briefly—and quietly and determinedly moved away. I barely had a glimpse. How did I respond? I immediately threw off my day-pack, bent over, and rifled for my camera. It was a unique opportunity, but I blew it. Instead of getting a better look at the mountain lion, I spent my time looking for my camera and bending over like some prospective prey. But I was young, a bit green, and did not know of any mountain lion attacks on humans, at least not in recent years.

Statistically, we are more in danger from others of our own kind than we are from wildlife. Ironically, we have come to accept elaborate safety precautions as a part of our lives, yet the same principles are not applied to wildlife. Central to safety in the big city, the basic safety practice of remaining aware and alert may also make the biggest difference with respect to mountain lions.

The management of mountain lions has always had a political history. For the greater part of this century, mountain lions were a "bountied" predator. These incentive-to-kill programs were subsidized by state and federal agencies to mitigate livestock losses and stimulate deer herd recoveries. At this time, towns only dotted the western landscape and livestock grazed over seemingly endless open range. Mountain lions were relatively common and a never-ending concern. The political resolve at the time was to eliminate them.

The bounty programs came to an end in the 1960s. After nearly 60 years, the programs' biological effectiveness and cost effectiveness were scrutinized, and the ethics of eliminating a large native member of the ecosystem were considered. Ironically, mountain lion populations persisted under these programs. Some scientists questioned whether these programs had resulted in any significant decrease in the predator populations that would allow an increase in deer herd numbers. State and federal agencies decided that it would be more cost effective to "target" and remove only those mountain lions that kill livestock. The mountain lion was further protected when it was added to the list of managed "game mammals," meaning the time, place, and number of animals killed would be regulated.

In the early 1970s new technology was developed, allowing us to monitor and study mountain lions at a level of precision that previously was not possible. Radio telemetry systems were developed for wildlife which were small and relatively affordable. For the first time, wildlife agencies and researchers could follow these animals over large distances and carefully determine activity centers and home range limits. Thanks to this technology, we have learned much more about the mountain lion's natural history. Although population estimates and home range measures derived before the 1970s are much less precise, mountain lions remain one of the most difficult large mammals in North America to study. Current efforts at monitoring with radio telemetry can be very costly and labor intensive.

Surprisingly, researchers have learned that mountain lions can range near people without ever being detected—a testament to the animal's stealth and wariness of humans. Unfortunately, attacks on people have become more frequent during the past 20 years. Attacks are still very rare, with only 1 to 5 attacks reported each year in North America. In California, for example, nearly all of the recent attacks have occurred in local, state, and county parks adjacent to larger metropolitan areas.

Conflicts will continue, as will the jeopardy of any mountain lion population in areas of significant habitat loss and fragmentation. Ironically, California voters established "special protection status" for mountain lions, yet failed to provide the needed funding to monitor populations and develop new conservation strategies.

There are no simple solutions. Although mountain lion hunting may not be a solution to public safety problems, neither is full protection of mountain lions. In the short run, perhaps the best we can do is continue to educate the public, resolve property and safety problems, and foster a balanced attitude toward predators.

"Conservation is a state of harmony between men and land," wrote Aldo Leopold in 1949. "Despite nearly a century of propaganda," he continued, "conservation still proceeds at a snail's pace; progress still consists largely of letterhead pieties and convention oratory. On the back forty we still slip two steps backward for each forward stride."

Therein lies the conservation dilemma. Change is certain, and the forecast for growth of human numbers in parts of the western United States and Canada is sobering. California's population is expected to increase by 50 percent, to almost 50 million people, by the year 2025. Projected development in the Central Valley of California and the nearby western slopes of the Sierra Nevada is staggering. Similar growth is forecast for many other western regions. In the long term, the challenge will be to assure the presence of mountain lions and their prey despite the certain loss of habitat and increases in human numbers and activity. Can this be done? The experiment is ongoing, and we may soon find out. Aldo Leopold's words point out the grim reality of implementing "conservation." However, his writings rightly encourage us to adopt a "land ethic" that understands and includes both public and private property owners—all advocates for wildlife and their habitats.

APPENDIX

Sources of Information

Although some of the following books are out of print, they can be found at a good library.

General Biology

Anderson, A. E. 1983. *A critical review of literature on puma* (felis concolor). Special Report No. 54. Denver: Colorado Division of Wildlife.

Halfpenny, J. 1986. *A field guide to mammal tracking in western America.* Boulder, Colo.: Johnson Books.

Hansen, K. 1992. *Cougar: the American lion.* N.p.: Northland Publishing.

Kitchner, A. 1991. *The natural history of the wild cats.* Ithaca, N.Y.: Comstock Publishing.

Logan, K. A., L. L. Sweanor, T. K. Ruth, and M. G. Hornocker. 1996. *Cougars of the San Andres Mountains, New Mexico.* Santa Fe: New Mexico Department of Game and Fish.

You can order this book by writing the New Mexico Department of Game and Fish, Division of Wildlife, Villagra Building, P.O. Box 25112, Santa Fe, New Mexico 87504. It costs $20. Make checks payable to the New Mexico Department of Game and Fish.

Murie, O. J. 1974. *A field guide to animal tracks.* Peterson Field Guide Series. New York: Houghton Mifflin.

Nowell, K. and P. Jackson, editors. 1996. *Wild cats: status survey and conservation action plan.* Cambridge, England: IUCN/SSC Cat Specialist Group.

You can order this book by writing the International Union for Conservation of Nature and Natural Resources, Publications Services Unit, 219c Huntingdon Road, Cambridge, CB3 ODL, United Kingdom. Or e-mail: IUCN-PSU@wcmc.org.uk.

Seidensticker, J. and S. Lumpkin, editors. 1991. *Great cats: majestic creatures of the wild.* Emmaus, Pa.: Rodale Press.

Shaw, H. 1989. *Soul among lions.* Boulder, Colo.:
Johnson Books.

Young, S. P., and E. A. Goldman. 1946. *The puma:
mysterious American cat.* Washington, D.C.:
American Wildlife Institute.

State and provincial fish and wildlife agencies also
produce management reports, special bulletins, and
safety brochures regarding mountain lions.

Attacks and Human Conflicts

Beier, P. 1991. Cougar attacks on humans in the
United States and Canada. *Wildlife Society
Bulletin.* 19: 403–12.

Torres, S. G., T. M. Mansfield, J. E. Foley, T. Lupo,
and A. Brinkhaus. 1996. Mountain lion and
human activity in California: testing speculations.
Wildlife Society Bulletin. 24: 451–60.

About the Author

Steven Torres has been studying wildlife in California and the Sonoran Desert of Arizona since 1980. He holds master's degrees in desert ecology and biostatistics from the University of Arizona and the University of California at Los Angeles, respectively. Since 1992, Steven has coordinated statewide research and management of both the mountain lion and bighorn sheep programs for the California Department of Fish and Game. His position provides him exposure to many different public attitudes toward mountain lions. His current mountain lion research focuses on habitat suitability and understanding factors influencing mountain lion–human conflicts.

Steven enjoys most every form of outdoor adventuring, but his favorites include looking for bighorn sheep, birdwatching, hunting, and canoeing and camping with his daughters Anna and Emily.

Hiking

Best Easy Day Hikes
  Canyonlands & Arches
Best Easy Day Hikes
  Yellowstone
Exploring Canyonlands &
  Arches National Parks
Hiking Alaska
Hiking Alberta
Hiking Arizona
Hiking Arizona's Cactus
  Country
Hiking the Beartooths
Hiking Big Bend National Park
Hiking California
Hiking California's Desert Parks
Hiking Carlsbad Caverns &
  Guadalupe Mountains
    National Parks
Hiking the Columbia
  River Gorge
Hiking Colorado
Hiking Florida
Hiking Georgia
Hiking Glacier and Waterton
  Lakes National Parks
Hiking Grand Canyon
  National Park
Hiking Hot Springs in the
  Pacific Northwest
Hiking Idaho
Hiking Maine
Hiking Michigan

Hiking Montana
The Hiker's Guide to Nevada
Hiking New Hampshire
Hiking New Mexico
Hiking New York
Hiking North Carolina
Hiking Northern Arizona
Hiking Olympic National Park
Hiking Oregon
Hiking Oregon's Eagle
  Cap Wilderness
Hiking Oregon's Three
  Sisters Country
Hiking South Dakota's Black
  Hills Country
Hiking Southern New England
Hiking Tennessee
Hiking Texas
Hiking Utah
Hiking Utah's Summits
Hiking Vermont
Hiking Virginia
Hiking Washington
Hiking Wyoming
Hiking Wyoming's Wind
  River Range
Hiking Yellowstone National Park
Hiking Zion & Bryce Canyon
  National Parks
The Trail Guide to Bob
  Marshall Country
Wild Montana